Ripley's Believe It or Not!®

WEIRD-ITIES!

Publisher Anne Marshall
Editorial Director Rebecca Miles
Assistant Editor Charlotte Howell
Text Geoff Tibballs
Proofreader Judy Barratt
Picture Researchers James Proud, Charlotte Howell
Art Director Sam South
Senior Designer Michelle Foster
Reprographics Juice Creative

Executive Vice President Norm Deska
Vice President, Archives and Exhibits Edward Meyer

PUBLISHER'S NOTE

While every effort has been made to verify the accuracy of the entries in this book, the Publishers cannot be held responsible for any errors contained in the work. They would be glad to receive any information from readers.

WARNING

Some of the stunts and activities in this book are undertaken by experts and should not be attempted by anyone without adequate training and supervision.

Published by Ripley Publishing 2013
Ripley Publishing, Suite 188, 7576 Kingspointe Parkway,
Orlando, Florida 32819, USA

2 4 6 8 10 9 7 5 3 1

ISBN 978-1-60991-026-6

Some of this material first appeared in *Ripley's Believe It or Not!*
Expect... The Unexpected

Library of Congress Cataloging-in-Publication data is available

Manufactured in China in February/2013 by Leo Paper
1st printing

Ripley's Believe It or Not!®

WEIRD-ITIES!

WEIRD AND WONDERFUL

Ripley
PUBLISHING
a Jim Pattison Company

PAGE
12

PAGE
15

WEIRD AND WONDERFUL

Against the odds. The most amazing art, outrageous festivals, and bizarre bodies are packed into this extraordinary book. Meet the father and son with six toes on each foot, the artist who paints by hearing colors, and the brave contestants at the Bug Eating Championships.

PAGE
26

PAGE
35

BREAD HEAD

Kittiwat Unarrom makes edible human heads and torsos out of dough! His workplace looks like a mortuary or a serial killer's dungeon, but it is in fact a bakery.

Visitors to Unarrom's workshop near Bangkok are alarmed to see the heads and torsos lined up on shelves, and rows of arms and hands hanging from meat hooks. The Thai art student, whose family runs a bakery, uses anatomy books and his memories of visiting a forensics museum to create the human body parts. In addition to heads crafted from bread, chocolate, raisins, and cashews, he makes human arms and feet, and chicken and pig parts, incorporating red food coloring for extra bloody effect. "When people see the bread, they don't want to eat it," he says. "But when they taste it, it's just normal bread. The lesson is, don't judge by appearances."

His macabre project started out as the centerpiece of his final dissertation for his Master of Arts degree, but as word spread about his novelty-shaped bread, regular orders began coming in from the curious or from pranksters who want to surprise their friends.

Basing the models on pictures from anatomy books, Thai art student Kittiwat Unarrom lovingly creates lifelike human heads from bread. Not surprisingly, most people think twice before eating the heads.

When customers first saw Kittiwat's room of realistic-looking human body parts, they were shocked and thought he was crazy.

Some of Kittiwat's creations are really gruesome and would not look out of place in a chamber of horrors. And if they're not bloody enough, he adds red food coloring to increase the effect.

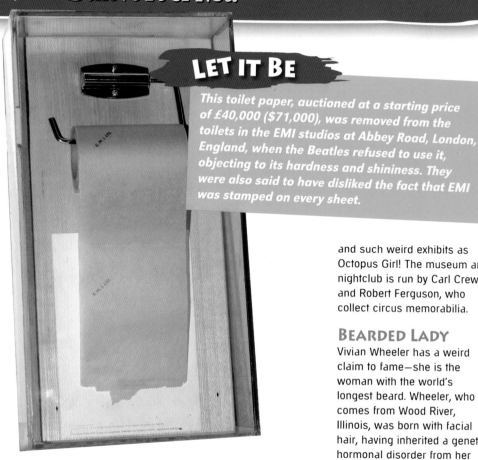

LET IT BE

This toilet paper, auctioned at a starting price of £40,000 ($71,000), was removed from the toilets in the EMI studios at Abbey Road, London, England, when the Beatles refused to use it, objecting to its hardness and shininess. They were also said to have disliked the fact that EMI was stamped on every sheet.

SELF-LIPOSUCTION
Believe it or not, Yugoslav-born plastic surgeon Dimitrije Panfilov performed liposuction on himself to remove his double chin!

TINY LETTERS
In 2004, physicists at Boston College, Massachussetts, managed to carve minuscule letters into a single strand of human hair. Using a laser, they created letters that were 15 micrometers tall. The technique can form items a thousand times smaller than the diameter of a human hair.

MIRACLE BIRTH
Nhlahla Cwayita was born healthy at Cape Town, South Africa, in 2003, despite developing in her mother's liver. She was only the fourth baby in the world to survive such a pregnancy.

CIRCUS CLUB
At one of the world's strangest nightclubs, the California Institute of Abnormalarts, you can dance the night away in the company of the remains of a dead clown, the stuffed carcass of a piglet-Chihuahua hybrid, a mummified arm, and such weird exhibits as Octopus Girl! The museum and nightclub is run by Carl Crew and Robert Ferguson, who collect circus memorabilia.

BEARDED LADY
Vivian Wheeler has a weird claim to fame—she is the woman with the world's longest beard. Wheeler, who comes from Wood River, Illinois, was born with facial hair, having inherited a genetic hormonal disorder from her mother. Her father refused to accept her beard and forced her to shave it off from the age of seven, but she later traveled with sideshow acts under the stage name of Melinda Maxie, dying her natural red hair black for greater impact. Her full beard has now reached a length of 11 in (28 cm), although she usually wears it tied up.

BEAD ART
Liza Lou of Topanga, California, used 40 million glass beads to create a kitchen and garden that was first displayed at the Kemper Museum of

ON A SHOESTRING

Big Bear City, California, is home to The Shoe Tree—no one quite knows how it started, but the tree continues to accumulate shoe upon shoe. Local police tried to prevent the tree being used in this way by removing all the shoes and fencing off the area, but by the next morning it was covered once again.

Contemporary Art in Kansas City in 1998. If the beads had been strung together, they would have stretched about 380 mi (610 km), the same distance as that between Los Angeles and San Francisco.

HOT STUFF

New Mexico State University has developed a special Halloween chili pepper, a miniature ornamental specimen that changes from black to orange. However,

Paul Bosland, head of the university's chili-breeding program, warns that these hot peppers are actually too hot to eat.

9

BIRD POOP

An American firm offers individually crafted models of birds made from genuine Californian horse dung!

FAKING FOR FUN

Chaucey Shea, of St. Catherine's, Ontario, Canada, has a potentially illegal hobby. He has mastered more than 2,000 forgeries of famous signatures, including English playwright William Shakespeare, and several presidents of the United States.

SEAT OF LEARNING

Bill Jarrett, a retired artist from Grand Rapids, Michigan, has been studying toilet paper for the past 30 years and now boasts a vast collection of tissue-related memorabilia.

TWO-FACED KITTEN

A kitten was born in Glide, Oregon, in June 2005, with two faces! Gemini astounded vets and owner Lee Bluetear with her two mouths, two tongues, two noses, and four eyes. Sadly, she died within a week.

SENTIMENTAL VALUE

Ezekiel Rubottom decided to keep his left foot after it was amputated in 2005! He stored it in the front porch of his Kansas home. After neigbors complained, he said "I'm not sick, I just wanted my foot."

WACKY WEDDING

At a wedding in Calgary, Alberta, Canada, in 1998, the bride was a sword swallower, the groom tamed bees, and the maid of honor made a living eating live bugs and worms! Megan Evans married Jim Rogers (Calgary's "Bee Man") in front of 200 musicians and freak-show performers, including worm-loving bridesmaid Brenda Fox.

SPLAT EXPERT

Mark Hostetler, an ecologist at the University of Florida, has written a book on how to identify insect splats left on your car. The book is titled *That Gunk On Your Car.*

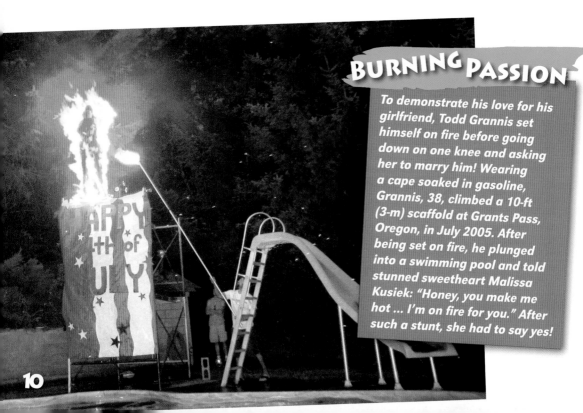

BURNING PASSION

To demonstrate his love for his girlfriend, Todd Grannis set himself on fire before going down on one knee and asking her to marry him! Wearing a cape soaked in gasoline, Grannis, 38, climbed a 10-ft (3-m) scaffold at Grants Pass, Oregon, in July 2005. After being set on fire, he plunged into a swimming pool and told stunned sweetheart Malissa Kusiek: "Honey, you make me hot ... I'm on fire for you." After such a stunt, she had to say yes!

HALF-SIZE JEANIE

Born without any legs, Jeanie Tomaini achieved fame in U.S. sideshows as "The Half Girl." While on tour, Jeanie, who is 2 ft 6 in (0.76 m), married Al, who stood 8 ft 4 in (2.54 m) tall and wore size 22 shoes. They went on to form a successful act as "The World's Strangest Couple."

OPEN WIDE

Jim Mouth, is a comedy entertainer based in Las Vegas who has been performing incredible stunts for more than 20 years. These often involve putting absolutely anything in his mouth!

When did you get started—and why do you keep going?

"My first stunt, when I was about 29, was playing drums for two weeks non stop. I had to drink lots of coffee to stay awake! My comedy shows are more of a full-time thing, but my biggest drive is to use stunts to raise money for charity."

What is your most famous stunt?

"I like doing the "most cigarettes in the mouth" stunt. I'm up to 159 cigarettes now. I've performed this on TV many times. I put all the cigarettes in apart from one which the host of the show puts in. Then they light them with two propane torches, I cough and wheeze for about three minutes, then spit them out. I'm dizzy for about half an hour afterward. One time I coughed out about 100 cigarettes—the crazy thing is I'm actually a non-smoker. I've actually done this stunt on non-smoking days to support people giving up cigarettes."

Do you have a special technique?

"Before a stunt I wedge corks into my mouth to stretch my lips, but my real secret is that I can dislocate my jaw. I didn't know I was doing it until they X-rayed me on a TV show last year. All I knew was that it was painful and made my eyes water!"

What other stunts do you do?

"Mouth stunts include smoking 41 cigars at once, and 41 pipes. We once had a whole band playing music under the water in a pool, and and another time I sat on every seat in the University of Michigan football stadium, the biggest in the U.S.A. There were 101,701 seats—it took me 96 hours 12 minutes, and four pairs of pants!"

How dangerous are your stunts?

"Apparently when my jaw dislocates it rests on my larynx, which could suffocate me. No one will insure me!"

Is there anything you would not do?

"Because I play drums I really don't want to break a finger or an arm. But I will put up with anything in my mouth—I might try keeping a tarantula spider in my mouth for half an hour."

How long will you carry on?

"My goal is to do one stunt every year for at least the next ten years. One I've got in the pipeline is "most hats on the head"—I'm aiming for a stack of 300, which will be about 8½ ft tall and weigh about 110 lb. I'll probably retire when I'm in my sixties—I'll do 170 cigarettes and then call it a day."

ASH ART

Bettye Jane Brokl incorporates the ashes of dead people into abstract paintings. The Biloxi, Mississippi, artist sprinkles the cremation ashes on the artwork to create a pictorial memorial for a loved one.

GERBIL INSTALLATION

An artist from Newcastle, England, made her pet gerbil the star of a 2005 exhibition. "The Gerbil's Guide to the Galaxy" showed Sally Madge's rodent chewing its way through a 1933 edition of the *New Illustrated Universal Reference Book*, "choosing" certain words to eat.

FIBERGLASS SHELL

A mud turtle that had its shell broken into eight pieces by cars in Lutz, Florida, was given a new fiberglass one in 1982.

JUNK EXHIBITION

In 2005, an exhibition in London, England, by Japanese artist Tomoko Takahashi featured 7,600 pieces of junk. The exhibits included old washing machines, broken toys, a rusty muck-spreader, and three stuffed blackbirds.

LOVE SHACK

In April 2005, a building was covered in 6,000 love letters, some penned by international celebrities, as part of the annual Auckland Festival in New Zealand.

MIND READER

Matthew Nagle, of Weymouth, Massachusetts, has a brain chip that reads his mind. Severely paralyzed after being stabbed in the neck in 2001, he has a revolutionary implant that enables him to control everyday objects simply by thinking about them. After drilling a hole into his head, surgeons implanted the chip a millimeter deep into his brain. Wafer-thin electrodes attached to the chip detect the electrical signals generated by his thoughts and relay them through wires into a computer. The brain signals are analyzed by the computer and translated into cursor movements. As well as operating a computer, software linked to other items in the room allows him to think his TV on and off and change channels.

SOARING SUCCESS

For her 1999 work "100 Ideas in the Atmosphere," Canadian performance artist Marie-Suzanne Désilets launched 100 helium balloons from the rooftop of a Montreal shopping mall with self-addressed notecards and an invitation to reply.

SLOW DINING

There's no fast food at June, a new restaurant in Lakewood Ranch, Florida. The nine-course meals take four hours to eat.

HEAD REATTACHED

Marcos Parra must be one of the luckiest guys alive. He survived a horrific car crash in 2002, in which his head was technically severed from the rest of his body. His skull was torn from his cervical spine, leaving his head detached from his neck. Only skin and his spinal cord kept the two body parts connected. Amazingly, however, surgeons in Phoenix, Arizona, managed to reattach his head. The bones were pulled into the right position by two screws placed at the back of his neck, enabling Parra to live.

MIRACLE HEART

Nikolai Mikhalnichuk leads a healthy life even though his heart stopped beating several years ago. He suffered a heart attack when his wife said she was leaving him, but doctors in Saratov, Russia, found that although his heart has stopped, its blood vessels are able to keep on pumping blood around his body.

BUSHY BROWS

In 2004, Frank Ames, of Saranac, New York State, had his eyebrow hair measured at an incredible 3.1 in (7.8 cm) long. Ames said "I don't know why it grows like that. It just always has."

EXTRA DIGITS

Filipinos Albert M. Perculeza and his son Karl Cedric each have 12 digits on their hands and 12 digits on their feet (see below). All 48 digits are fully functional.

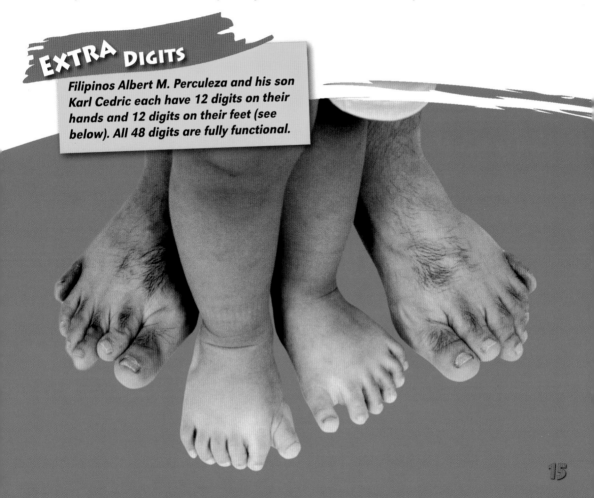

HUMAN SOAP

A bar of soap that was said to have been made from body fat pumped from the Italian Prime Minister Silvio Berlusconi sold for almost $20,000 in 2005. Artist Gianni Motti said that he acquired the fat from a private Swiss clinic where Berlusconi reportedly underwent liposuction. Motti said the fat was "jelly-like and stunk horribly."

HAM ACTORS

Father and son, Olivier and Yohann Roussel, won one of Europe's most coveted prizes in 2005—the French Pig-squealing Championships. Dressed in pig outfits, the Roussels impressed the judges and spectators with squeals, grunts, and snuffles to represent the four key stages of a pig's life—birth, suckling, mating, and death under the knife.

BLIND DIAGNOSIS

Dr. James T. Clack, of Wadley, Alabama, treated patients in the 1940s even though he was blind.

HARDY EATER

"Hungry" Charles Hardy, of Brooklyn, New York, describes himself as "the Michael Jordan of competitive eating." In 2001, he ate 23 hot dogs in 12 minutes, and also became Matzo Ball Eating world champion. But his talent has drawbacks. Hardy explains: "I found a place in Manhattan with all-you-can-eat sushi for $19.95. When the lady sees me coming, she hits the clock and gives me one and a half hours."

HEART BEAT

Jeweler Didier Verhill, of Antwerp, Belgium, creates wedding rings engraved with the couple's heartbeat pattern taken from a cardiograph!

SNEEZY PLATE

Allergist Dr. Edwin Dombrowski, of Stamford, Connecticut, had the automobile licence plate "AH-CHoo."

ZERO INFLATION

Dr. Anna Perkins, of Westerloo, New York, charged the same rates in 1993 that she had set in 1928: $4 for an office visit, $5 for a house call, and $25 to deliver a baby.

SELL-OUT FUNERAL

When Dr. William Price, of Llantrisant, south Wales, died in 1893, more than 6,000 tickets were sold for his public cremation, as specified in his will.

BUTTON KING

Dalton Stevens, of Hartsville, South Carolina, has fixed an incredible 600,000 buttons to his Pontiac hearse. Another 60,000 buttons cover the coffin inside! Besides the hearse, he has shoes, musical instruments, and even a toilet covered with buttons.

WRIST-BREAKER

That K.S. Raghavendra, from India, is capable of breaking 13 eggs in 30 seconds doesn't sound amazing in itself, except he doesn't break them by clenching his fist, but by bending his hand back over his wrist.

TOBACCO MOUTH

Prince Randian, known as "The Living Torso," had no arms or legs. However, he amazingly learned to roll, light, and smoke a cigarette by moving his mouth.

FOUR-LEGGED WOMAN

Myrtle Corbin, the four-legged woman from Texas, had a malformed Siamese twin, which resulted in Myrtle having two pairs of legs. She used to gallop across the stage like a horse.

SNOWBALL FLAG

In 1998, Vasili Mochanou, of Ottawa, Ontario, created a replica of the Canadian Flag using 27,000 snowballs!

TWO-SIDED

Edward Mordrake was born a Siamese twin, and had another face on the reverse of his—that of a beautiful girl whose eyes used to follow you around the room.

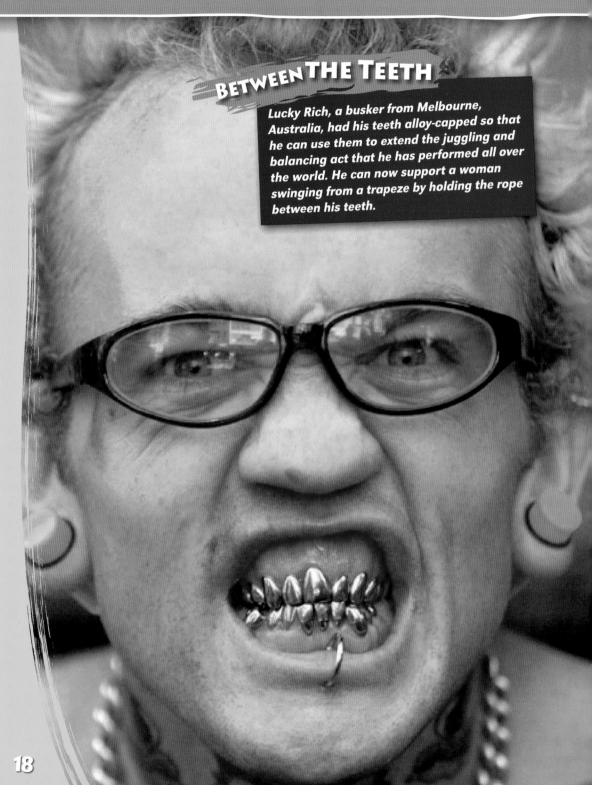

BETWEEN THE TEETH

Lucky Rich, a busker from Melbourne, Australia, had his teeth alloy-capped so that he can use them to extend the juggling and balancing act that he has performed all over the world. He can now support a woman swinging from a trapeze by holding the rope between his teeth.

FREE PIG

In an unusual bid to boost sales in 2005, an entrepreneurial British housing developer offered a free gift of a live pig to anyone who bought a property from him. Jeremy Paxton, who is based in Gloucestershire, England, promised that the rare breed Gloucester Old Spot pigs would be fully house-trained before delivery.

GIANT RODENT

For a 2004 art festival, Dutchman Florentun Hofman built a sculpture of a beaver 100 ft (31 m) long and 25 ft (8 m) high, using just wood and reeds. The year before, he created a 37-ft (11-m) high rabbit.

NOSE GROWN

Madina Yusuf had her face reconstructed by growing a new nose on her arm. The Nigerian woman was severely disfigured by a flesh-eating disease that left her without a nose and with very little mouth. But, in 2001, she flew to Aberdeen, Scotland, where Dr. Peter Ayliffe grafted her new nose from extra skin grown on her arm, plus bone and cartilage that had been taken from her right rib.

ASTRAL GROOMING

Astronauts in space shave using razors equipped with tiny vacuum cleaners inside!

BALLOON SCULPTURE

U.S. balloon sculptor Larry Moss used more than 40,000 balloons to construct a model of two football players at Mol, Belgium, in 2000. Each player was 40 ft (12 m) tall.

THE SMELL OF ITALY

In 2003, Ducio Cresci, of Florence, Italy, created a series of bathroom products— including soap, lotion, and bubble bath—that smelled just like pizza!

TINY TACKLER

The ace defence tackler on the football team at Flint Southwestern Academy High School, Michigan, was only 3 ft (0.9 m) tall, having been left with no legs after a 1994 railroad accident. Willie McQueen earned his place on the team by courage and tenacity. He didn't play in a wheelchair or wear prostheses, but scooted around to create havoc in the opposing backfield.

GARBAGE TOUR

In Chicago in 2005, people were paying $7 to see some of the city's less desirable spots on a three-hour bus tour of garbage sites, landfills, and smelly sludge sewage fields. The excursion showed residents and visitors what happens to garbage once it leaves their trash cans.

LOBSTER FEET

The fingers of this unidentified man from upstate western New York have mutated to look like lobster claws. This was the result of inbreeding.

ELASTIC MAN

Dubbed "Mr Elastic," Moses Lanham can turn his feet around 180 degrees, completely backwards, and then walk in the opposite direction!

Lanham puts his unique talent down to being born with extra ligaments and cartilage within the joints of his ankles, knees, and hips, which enable him to rotate his bones freely within the sockets of his joints.

Amazingly, he didn't realize he had this ability until he suffered a fall in gym class at the age of 14 and landed awkwardly. Jumping to his feet, he suddenly found that he could easily twist both of his feet around backward. Lanham, from Monroe, Michigan, has discovered that his son Trey also appears to have inherited the extra joint tissue. At 11, he can turn his feet backward just like his dad! "He can't walk backwards yet," says Moses, "but he is learning."

Moses enjoys putting his best foot backwards, and often performs at local fund-raising events.

Moses Lanham's body contains extra joint tissue that enables him to turn his feet backwards. Moses can even walk backwards too!

OUR LADY OF THE UNDERPASS

Thousands of worshipers flocked to a Chicago underpass in April 2005 and created a shrine of candles and flowers, after a watery mark on the concrete wall was interpreted as an image of the Virgin Mary. Visitors touched and kissed the mark, which was thought to have been caused by salt running down from the Kennedy Expressway overhead. However, the devout insisted it was a miracle that had appeared in order to mark the death of Pope John Paul II.

LEDGER BALANCING

Balancing ledgers while balancing on ledges or deep-sea diving with a tax return are just some ways to perform Extreme Accounting. First established by Arnold Chiswick, the extreme sport incorporates everything involved in an accounting desk job with the added thrill of sporting action.

SPECIES FOR SALE

A new species of rodent was discovered in 2005—for sale on a food stall in a market in Laos. The rock rat, or kha-nyou, was spotted by conservation biologist Robert Timmins who knew it was something he'd never seen before. The animal looks like a cross between a rat and a squirrel, but is not actually related to any other rodents at all.

SNAKE DIET

Neeranjan Bhaskar claims to have eaten more than 4,000 snakes, including deadly cobras. Bhaskar, who is otherwise vegetarian, hunts for snakes every morning on the banks of the Ghagra River near his home in India. He first ate a snake at the age of seven.

SKIN HORROR

After being prescribed a common antibiotic to treat a routine sinus infection in 2003, Sarah Yeargain, from San Diego, California, looked on in horror as her skin began peeling away in sheets. With Sarah's condition—caused by a severe allergic reaction to the drug—getting worse, more of her skin came off in her mother's hands as she was carried into a hospital. She eventually lost the skin from her entire body—including her internal organs and the membranes covering her mouth, throat, and eyes. Doctors gave her no chance of survival, but they covered her body in an artificial skin replacement and within a few days her own skin returned.

DOG DIVER

When Dwane Folsom went scuba diving, his dog went too! Folsom, from Boynton Beach, Florida, designed the first scuba-diving outfit for dogs, comprising a lead-weighted jacket, a helmet, and a tube that allowed the animal to draw air from the human diver's tank. Folsom and his dog, named Shadow, regularly dived to depths of 13 ft (4 m).

HOLY SHOWER

In 2005, Jeffrey Rigo, of Pittsburgh, Pennsylvania, sold a water stain on his bathroom wall for nearly $2,000 because he considered that it bore a resemblance to Jesus. Following the publicity for the "Shower Jesus," Rigo had requests from people who wanted to pray in his bathtub.

HIDDEN MONKEYS

When Californian Robert Cusack was asked if he had anything to declare on arrival at Los Angeles Airport in 2002, customs officers could hardly have expected what they would find. They discovered a pair of pygmy monkeys in his pants and a bird of paradise in his suitcase. Cusack was subsequently sentenced to 57 days in jail for smuggling the monkeys, as well as four exotic birds, and 50 rare orchids into the U.S. all the way from Thailand.

EMERGENCY REPAIRS

Jonas Scott, from Salt Lake City, Utah, was left with no esophagus after industrial cleaning fluid at his workplace ate away his insides in 1988. With no stomach, he had to be fed intravenously. He went three years without eating solids until surgeons connected the remaining 7 ft (2.1 m) of his small intestine directly to the base of his throat so that he could eat almost normally again.

AMBIDEXTROUS BILINGUIST

In 2004, Amanullah, a 53-year-old man from India, learned to write different sentences simultaneously with both hands. Most amazing of all, he could write one sentence in English, and the other in Tamil.

GREAT BALLS OF FIRE!

Stonehenge in Wiltshire, England, was the location for a massive synchronized fire-eating spectacular. Seventy fire-eaters came together to create a landscape of flames at the event in September 2004.

PULLING POWER

The Great Nippulini can tow a car from the piercings attached to his nipples, as well as lift a phenomenal 55 lb (25 kg).

TURTLE RECALL

In 2005, a Chinese man pretended to be a hunchback in order to smuggle his pet turtle onto a plane. The elderly man strapped the turtle, which was 8 in (20 cm) in diameter, to his back before boarding a flight to Chongqing, but after getting through security, he was stopped by a guard who thought his hump looked strange.

FANCY DRESS

The first prize in the youth division of the July 4 Parade in Haines, Oregon, in 2005, went to three children dressed as dung beetles! Wearing tubes covered by garbage bags, they pushed huge rubber balls coated in sand, dirt, and dead grass.

LIVE BY THE SWORD

New Yorker Natasha Veruschka, claims to be the world's only belly-dancing sword swallower, and defies a strict religious upbringing to risk her life for her passion.

When did you first become fascinated by swords?

"My British mother died when I was two. I don't remember my Siberian father—I was adopted into a strict Mennonite family in southern Ukraine. I wasn't allowed to hear music, or look in a mirror, or cut my hair. When I was four I saw a knife in a church—I was mesmerized. I remember putting the tip of it on my tongue to feel it."

How did your act begin?

"I grew up in countries including India, Egypt, and Iran, and later took belly dancing lessons in New York. I learned sword balancing, but one night I ended a performance by kissing the sword—I realized then that I wanted to be a sword swallower. The first time I did it, nine years ago, it felt like home—it made me complete."

What kinds of swords do you swallow?

"The longest is 27 ½ inches— which is a lot because I am only 5 ft 4 in tall and weigh just over 100 lb. I have 25 different swords—including a Sai sword, which is an eight-sided Japanese war weapon. I can swallow up to 13 swords at once."

Which is the most dangerous?

"The neon sword, which is filled with poisonous gas and is so fragile that your stomach muscles can shatter it inside you. It is electric and heats up—one time, it started to burn and adhere to my insides. Since 1942, six people have died swallowing one."

Have you ever cut yourself on a sword?

"Once I nearly died—I lost 53 per cent of my blood. I had three swords inside me and a man pushed me. The blades scissored and cut my lower esophagus. After the show, I was vomiting blood everywhere and even had a near-death experience. They told me at the hospital that I would be in the morgue by the following morning. I was back swallowing swords within a month."

Where does the sword go?

"To the bottom of the stomach. I can swallow a chocolate cherry, put a sword down, and bring it back up. You have to overcome much more than a gag reflex—the sword has to go past two muscle sphincters as well, on its way past the lungs and heart."

Do you have any special techniques?

"I say a prayer before every performance, and use yoga to go into 'a zone.' I use no lubricant, no special tubes. You need a lot of upper body strength—the swords weigh close to 12 ½ lb when I swallow them all at once— and a lot of lung capacity. It's not magic. I have been X-rayed and you can see the sword in me. The neon one glows through my body for all to see."

What drives you—and how long will you do this?

"My family have shunned me for what I do. To them, I am dead. I think this all stems from an 'I'll show you' attitude. As for how long, I won't be happy until I'm the oldest female belly-dancing sword swallower in the world!"

27

MINI COWS

In an attempt to combat his country's serious milk shortage of 1987, Fidel Castro urged his scientists to create a breed of mini cows. Castro wanted the most productive cows cloned and shrunk to the size of dogs so that families could keep one inside their apartments. There, the cows would feed on grass grown under fluorescent lights.

PECULIAR PASTIMES

In Rieti, Italy, there is an annual washtub race in which contestants race wooden washtubs along a course 875 yd (800 m) long.

EXTREME CARVING

In Port Elgin, Ontario, Canada, there is an annual pumpkin festival that includes such unique events as underwater pumpkin carving.

BUSSE LOAD

When the Busse family marked the 150th anniversary of the arrival of their ancestors in the U.S.A. from Germany, it was no ordinary reunion: 2,369 family members turned up at Grayslake, Illinois, in 1998, some from as far away as Africa.

COMPETITIVE KITE-FLYING

Kite fighting is common at the spring Festival of Basant in Lahore, Pakistan. Skilled kite-flyers from all around the country use bladed and chemical-lined strings to bring down or capture their opponents' kites.

SPACE ODDITY

Canadian performance artist Julie Andrée T. sought to redefine space by walking blindfold in a confined space for six hours, marking the walls and singing a children's song.

TWO NOSES

Bill Durks was born in 1913 with two noses, each with a single nostril. Between the bridges of his noses, he painted a third eye, over what may have been a vestigial eye socket, and became known in U.S. sideshows as "The Man with Three Eyes." He married Milly Durks, "The Alligator-skinned Woman From New Jersey."

WRAPPERS REBORN

Finnish artist Virpi Vesanen-Laukkanen exhibited this dress, in St. Petersburg, Russia, made entirely of candy wrappers. The artist said that her creation reminded her of sweets eaten during long journeys.

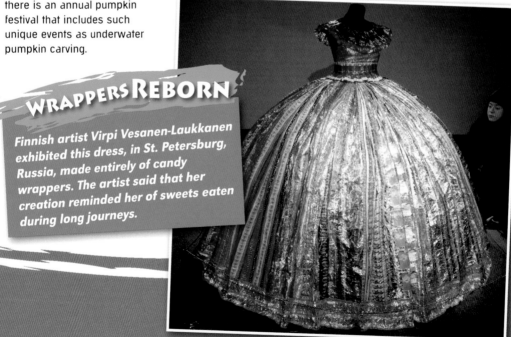

HUGE HALLOWEEN

Belgian artist Michel Dircken sits in his carving, created during a competition for the fastest carving of a jack o'lantern in October 2005. The pumpkin weighed 637 lb (289 kg) and measured 131 in (333 cm) around.

BIRTH ART

As part of an exhibition in a German art gallery, a woman gave birth in front of dozens of spectators. Ramune Gele had the baby girl, named Audra, in 2005, at the DNA gallery in Berlin. The father, Winfried Witt, called the experience "an existential work of art."

TOE THUMB

After Peter Morris, from Kingswinford, England, lost his thumb in a 1993 accident, doctors replaced it with his big toe.

SEWN EAR

Trampled by a bull in 1993, Jim McManus, of Calgary, Canada, had his left ear reattached by doctors—aided by 75 leeches to help control the bleeding.

29

FYRE EATER

Eating fire, swallowing swords, juggling machetes, hammering nails up his own nose—they're all in a day's work for the Amazing Blazing Tyler Fyre!

Fyre (real name Tyler Fleet), born in Georgia, was a one-off even as a kid, when he found that he could squirt milk, water, and even spaghetti and meatballs out of his nose. He learned trapeze, juggling, balancing, the high wire, and fire-eating, before progressing to a routine as a Human Blockhead. In ten years, Fyre, who also eats glass, razor blades, live crickets, and lit cigarettes, and has been known to pound a nail through a hole in his tongue, has done more than 7,500 live shows, sometimes performing 15 a day. He admits: "It's grueling on the body. At the Coney Island Circus Sideshow I was the Human Blockhead, the sword swallower, I ate fire, and I did the inverted escape act, cranked up by my ankles until my head was 6 ft above the stage."

When it comes to swallowing swords, Tyler's act puts him at the cutting edge of show business.

Tyler used to hammer a nail through the hole in his tongue. He still enjoys putting toothpicks in it.

In a daring escapology routine, Tyler is tied in a straitjacket and hung upside down by his ankles 6 ft (1.8 m) above the stage.

THROUGH THE NOSE

Jin Guolong, from China, can drink through his nose—he consumes both milk and alcohol using this method.

KILLER TREE

In 1860, nearly 200 years after his death, the Rhode Island Historical Society exhumed the body of Roger Williams—only to find that he had been eaten by an apple tree! The coffin was empty apart from the invading tree roots. A large root curved where his head should have been and entered the chest cavity before growing down the spine. It then branched at the two legs and upturned into feet.

ICE SCULPTOR

Richard Bubin, aged 44, from Wilkins, Pennsylvania, has been sculpting ice for more than 20 years and once carved 61 blocks in under 4½ hours. For Pittsburgh's First Night celebration in January 2005, he turned ten giant blocks of ice into a sculpture of the Roberto Clemente Bridge.

JUMBO JUNK

British artist Anthony Heywood made a full-size elephant sculpture in 2004 entirely from household junk, including TV sets, heaters, fans, radios, and a toilet.

STAIR RIDE

In the 2005 urban Down the Hill bike race, held in the town of Taxco, Mexico, competitors rode their mountain bikes through a house! They went in through a door, down a flight of stairs and exited through another door. They also sped through narrow alleys and jumped heights of 13 ft (4 m) on the 2-mi (3.2-km) course.

LEGGED IT!

A man testing an artificial leg worth $17,000 ran off without paying the bill. The theft occurred after the man called in to collect a prosthetic from a specialist in Des Moines, Iowa, in 2005, and was allowed to take it away for a couple of hours to ensure that it fitted him properly.

CHICKEN PROTEST

Ottawa performance artist Rob Thompson caged a man and a woman in 1997 to protest about the conditions of commercially bred chickens. Eric Wolf and Pam Meldrum spent a week together in the small wooden cage to make the point. Their drinking water came from a dripping hose and they ate vegetarian mash.

LOVE BIRDS

During the Middle Ages, people in Europe are said to have believed that birds chose their mates every year on Valentine's Day!

X-RAY EYES

A teenage Russian girl appears to have X-ray vision, which enables her to see inside human bodies. Natalia Demkina has baffled scientists across the world by describing the insides of bodies in detail and using her talent to correctly diagnose the medical conditions of complete strangers. She says that she possesses dual vision when looking at others, but that she can't see inside her own body. Natalia switches from normal to X-ray vision by focusing on a person for two minutes.

PRETTY AS A PICTURE

A participant in the 13th International Tattoo Convention, held in Frankfurt, Germany, in 2005, sports a tattoo on the back of his head.

MINI MARRIAGE

In 1863, "General Tom Thumb," or Charles Stratton, married Lavinia Warren. Lavinia was heralded as a miniature of perfect proportions, and the marriage was a major event in New York society.

PET PILLOWS

In 2005, Nevada taxidermist Jeanette Hall offered to make fur pillows from dead pets. Each Pet Pillow was handmade for prices ranging from $65 for a cat to $150 for a horse. Hall described the idea as a "unique way of keeping your pets close to you even after they pass away."

CRICKET LOVER

Danny Capps, of Madison, Wisconsin, spits dead crickets from his mouth over distances of up to 30 ft (9 m). Capps, who has been fascinated by insects since he was a small boy, says that dead crickets have no flavor.

SHOPPING BREAK

Tired shoppers in Minnesota's Mall of America can rest their weary legs for 70 cents a minute. In the Bloomington shopping center there is a store called MinneNAPolis aimed at bored spouses of shoppers and also at travelers, who need a nap after a lengthy flight, but aren't staying long enough to book a hotel.

PAVEMENT PICASSO

Ben Wilson roams the streets of London, England, looking for used chewing gum, which he turns into works of art. He burns the gum with a blowtorch, adds a clear enamel as a base, then colors in acrylic enamels, and finishes with a coat of varnish. His gum gallery includes human portraits, animals, and buildings.

PREGNANT BOY

When seven-year-old Alamjan Nematilaev's tummy began to bulge, his parents thought he had rickets, a common childhood disease in his native Kazakhstan. But, in 2003, a concerned schoolteacher took him to hospital, where doctors removed a 4-lb (1.8-kg) baby boy from Alamjan's stomach! Alamjan had been born with the fetus of his twin brother growing inside him. For seven years it had lived like a parasite, growing a head, a body, hair, and nails. Doctors were able to save Alamjan but not the 8-in (20-cm) fetus.

WALL EATER

In 2005, Emily Katrencik ate through the wall of her Brooklyn gallery until she could put her head through it—all in the name of art. She said: "The wall has a mild flavor. The texture is more prominent than the taste—it's chalky with tiny sharp pieces in it." Visitors to the gallery could eat bread made with minerals extracted from the wall.

FROG BIRTH

A woman from Iran was reported to have given birth to a gray frog-like creature in 2004. It apparently grew from a larva that had entered the woman as she swam in a dirty pool. A doctor described the creature as resembling a frog in appearance, particularly the shape of the fingers, and the size and shape of the tongue.

IN FOND MEMORY

Swedish artist and sculptor Lars Widenfalk has created a violin with a difference. He sculpted the working instrument from the tombstone of his late grandfather, Gustav. The violin's fingerboard, pegs, tailpiece, and chin rest are all made of ebony, and by lining the interior with real gold, it produces the finest possible tone. The instrument is considered to be worth in the region of $1.7 million.

TALON CONTEST

Louise Hollis, of Compton, California, has let her toenails grow to a staggering 6 in (15 cm) long. She has to wear open-toed shoes with at least 3-in (7.6-cm) soles to stop her nails dragging along the ground, and she needs 2½ bottles of nail polish to paint the nails on both her hands and feet.

PAN CHRIST

As Juan Pastrano, of Prairie Lea, Texas, was hanging up his frying pan after washing it in 2005, he spotted an uncanny image where the anti-stick coating on the pan had worn thin. There before him was the face of Jesus Christ in a crown of thorns. He promptly sealed the pan in a plastic bag to protect the image from curious visitors.

TOOTHY FOOT

Teenager Doug Pritchard, of Lenoir, North Carolina, went to his doctor in 1978 with a sore foot. Amazingly a tooth was found growing in the bottom of his instep!

THORNY LANDING

Jens Jenson, of Denmark, fell into a pile of spiky barberries in 1990 and had to visit his doctor 248 times to have a total of 32,131 thorns removed from his punctured body.

SMALL WONDER

Ma Chaoqin, from China, is 22 years old, but still looks like a baby. She suffers from an incurable disease called Rachitic, or rickets, and as a result has failed to grow at a normal rate.

HEARING IN COLORS

Color-blind art student Neil Harbisson wears a special device that enables him to "hear" colors.

Neil, from Spain, uses a device called the Eye-Borg, that was invented by Adam Montandon, a digital multimedia expert from Plymouth, England. It works by converting light waves into sounds, and consists of a digital camera and a backpack that contains the computer and headset for Neil to listen to the colors. A low-pitched sound indicates reds, a high-pitched sound indicates violet, while shades of blue and green fall somewhere in between.

Now Neil, who takes off the invention only when he sleeps, is able to buy clothes that he "likes the sound of." He can also order his favorite foods, whereas previously he struggled to differentiate between apple juice and orange juice.

> **When Neil first applied for a passport and sent a photo of himself wearing the camera, it was rejected. "So I sent a letter to the passport office explaining that I was a cyborg. They accepted me as a cyborg."**

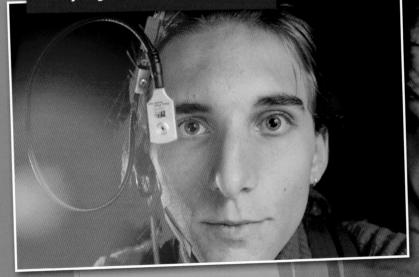

Neil now paints in vibrant colors.

SNAKE MAN

For more than 50 years, Bill Haast injected himself with deadly snake venom. He built up such powerful antibodies in his system that his blood was used as a snakebite antidote. Haast, who ran a Florida serpentarium, began in 1948 with tiny amounts of rattlesnake venom and built up the dosage until, by the time he was 90, he was injecting himself once a week with venom from 32 species. Although he was bitten more than 180 times by snakes from which a few drops of venom could kill any ordinary human, Haast managed to survive every single time.

TWO HEARTS

A boy in Tbilisi, Georgia, was born with two hearts. In 2004, doctors discovered that one-year-old Goga Diasamidze had been born with a second perfectly functioning heart near his stomach.

SNAIL TRAIL

In Januray 2005, Chilean artist Paola Podesta promoted her new exhibition by gluing 2,000 plastic snails to a Santiago church. The snail trail led from the Church of Santo Expedito to the nearby Codar art gallery.

OMELET SURPRISE

When Ursula Beckley, of Long Island, New York, was preparing an omelette in 1989, she cracked open an egg— only to see a 6-in (15-cm) black snake slither out. She sued her local supermarket for $3.6 million on the grounds that she was so traumatized by the incident that she could never look at an egg again.

POOPER SCOOPER

Steve Relles makes a living by scooping up dog poop! The Delmar Dog Butler, as he calls himself, has more than 100 clients in New York State who pay $10, each for a weekly clean of their yard.

ROBOT RIDERS

In 2005, Qatar, in the Middle East, staged a spectacular camel race using robot jockeys. Seven robots were placed on top of seven camels at Al Shahaniyya racecourse, near the country's capital Doha, after there had been widespread protests about the use of children as jockeys in the popular sport.

SENSITIVE SHIRT

Italian designer Francesca Rosella has come up with the perfect gift for people involved in long-distance relationships—a hugging T-shirt. Fitted with sensors, the T-shirt simulates the missing partner's caress by recreating breath, touch, and heartbeat based on information transmitted to the T-shirt via their cell phone.

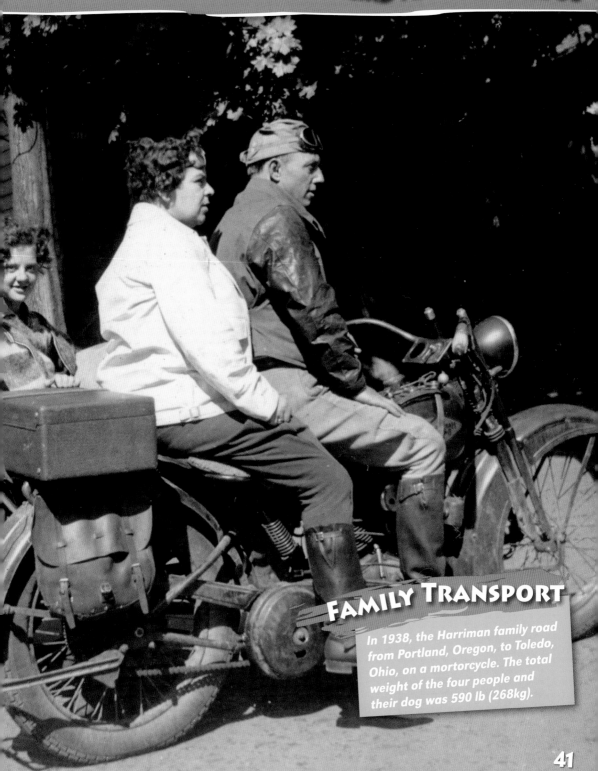

FAMILY TRANSPORT

In 1938, the Harriman family road from Portland, Oregon, to Toledo, Ohio, on a mortorcycle. The total weight of the four people and their dog was 590 lb (268kg).

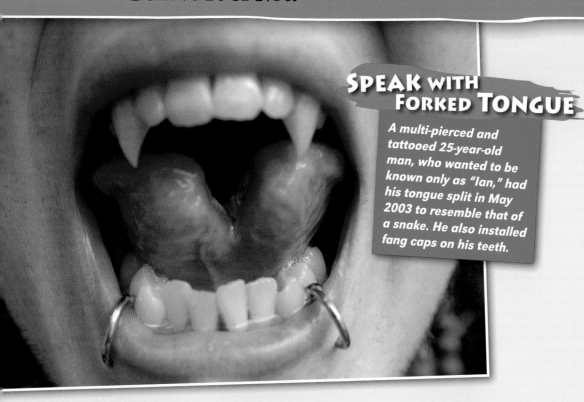

SPEAK WITH FORKED TONGUE

A multi-pierced and tattooed 25-year-old man, who wanted to be known only as "Ian," had his tongue split in May 2003 to resemble that of a snake. He also installed fang caps on his teeth.

FISH BONES

Chinese artist Liu Huirong recreates famous works of art in fish bones! She took two years and used more than 100,000 fish bones to complete a copy of "Spring's Back," a 300-year-old painting by Yuan Jiang. She has been making fish-bone pictures for more than 20 years. Every day she collects fish bones from roadside garbage bins and degreases, marinates, and chemically treats them before sticking them on to canvas.

BRANCHING OUT

For more than 25 years, performance artist David "The Bushman" Johnson has been alarming people on Fisherman's Wharf, San Francisco, by jumping out from behind branches as they pass by. He has been arrested over 1,000 times as a result of people not getting the joke.

BONE SCULPTURE

In 2001, U.S. artist Sarah Perry created "Beast of Burden," a 9-ft (2.7-m) rocketship made from horse and cattle bones! She has created other sculptures from hundreds of tiny rodent bones, which she has painstakingly extracted from owl pellets. She also makes art using junk that has been discarded in the Nevada Desert and once made a 700-lb (318-kg) gorilla from old rubber truck-tires.

RAW TALENT

Gabriela Rivera horrified visitors to an art gallery in Santiago, Chile, in 2005, by showing a video of herself with her face covered in raw meat. She said it showed the relationship people have with themselves each day when they look in the mirror.

WINTER WOOLLIES

In 2001, a group of volunteers in Tasmania, Australia, knitted turtleneck sweaters for a colony of rare Australian penguins to protect the birds against oil spills!

HAIR FORCE

Indian police have been trying to improve their public image by paying officers to grow mustaches. In 2004, chiefs in Madhya Pradesh announced a monthly mustache bonus of 30 rupees (about 50 cents) after research showed that officers with smart facial hair were taken more seriously. Mustaches are a sign of authority in India.

GHOSTLY PAYOUT

In 2001, an insurance company in Great Britain offered a "Spooksafe" policy for death, injury, or damage caused by a ghost or poltergeist.

TIME CAPSULE

At the 1957 Tulsarama Festival in Tulsa, Oklahoma, a brand new Chrysler car was buried in a time capsule, to be unearthed in 2007. People were asked to guess Tulsa's population in 2007. Whoever is closest wins the car; if that person is dead, the heirs get the car.

OVER YOUR HEAD

Shanghai, in China, saw the première of what was billed as the first acrobatic ballet—a combination of Western dance and ancient Chinese acrobatics. In this scene from "Swan Lake the Acrobatic," a ballerina balanced on her toes on the head of a male dancer.

IN A TWIST

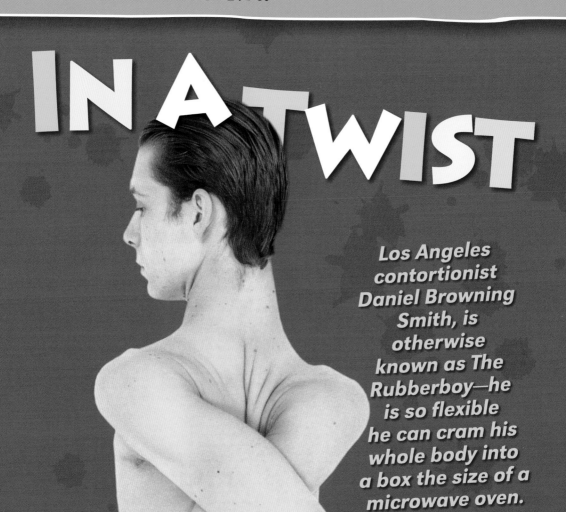

Los Angeles contortionist Daniel Browning Smith, is otherwise known as The Rubberboy—he is so flexible he can cram his whole body into a box the size of a microwave oven.

When did you first discover your flexibility?

"I was four years old when I jumped off my bunk bed and landed in a perfect saddle split. I showed my father and he went to the library and brought me home pictures of contortionists—I tried to copy them, and I could. As a kid playing hide and seek I could hide in the sock drawer!"

How did you turn that into a career?

"When I was 18 the circus came through town where I grew up in Mississippi. I told my family I was joining it and would be back in three weeks—that was eight years ago."

What exactly can you do?

"I believe I am the most flexible person alive. Most contortionists can only bend one way—I can bend so far backwards the top of my head touches the seat of my pants, and so far forward I can kiss my own behind! I can also disconnect both arms, both legs, and turn my torso 180 degrees."

What is your favorite stunt?

"De-Escape—it is the complete opposite of Houdini's straitjacket routine. I have to dislocate my arms and squeeze into a locked straitjacket, then chain myself up with my mouth and flip myself into a box."

What else can you do?

"I can make my ribcage go up and my abdomen go down so you can see my heart beating through my skin! And I can get into a box about the size of a microwave. I get my shins in first, because I can't bend them, then my back, then my head and arms fill the holes. I have to slow down my breathing because my arms and legs put pressure on my lungs."

Does it hurt?

"I practice a stretch until just before it becomes painful, then hold it a bit until it feels normal, then stretch a bit further. The connective tissue between my bones is different genetically, inherited from both sides of my family. My father's father was in the military and it helped him to dislocate his hips when it was time to march. The stretches I do enhance that for me."

Have you ever got stuck?

"I can get through an unstrung tennis racquet or a toilet seat, but once a toilet seat got stuck around my torso with my thigh in the hole as well. I was home alone, and had to crawl into the kitchen and get a bottle of vegetable oil and pour it all over me. The seat finally came off—I just made a huge mess."

Are you working on future stunts?

"I'm trying to turn my head 180 degrees. I can get to about 175 degrees already. It's the only thing I've tried that's made me gasp—it's weird looking down and seeing your own butt!"

ROCK AROUND THE CLOCK

Thirty-six-year-old Suresh Joachim, from Mississauga, Ontario, spent 3 days 3 hours 3 minutes 3 seconds rocking in a rocking chair nonstop in August 2005. In the course of his challenge at the Hilton Garden Inn, Toronto, Ontario, he ate just one plain white bun, some noodle soup, three hard-boiled eggs, and one and a half potatoes. He also drank water and energy drinks, but not enough so that he would have to go to the toilet. His greatest fear was falling asleep, because of the need to rock continuously back and forth.

BLOOD STAINS

Mexican artist Teresa Margolles staged a 2005 exhibition in Metz, France, featuring clothing stained with human blood. She worked in a morgue for ten years and her display comprised clothes worn by corpses.

HAIR WEAR

Nina Sparre, of Vamhuf, Sweden, practices the art of Haarkulla, or "Hair Farming," creating art and clothing out of human hair!

LIVING BILLBOARD

Forty models lived in a 3-D billboard on the side of a building for two days in July 2005, creating New York City's first-ever live billboard. They were advertising a new fragrance from Calvin Klein. The models were told to create an illusion of a big party, 24 hours a day.

LAST RIDE OF YOUR LIFE!

Gordon Fitch took his passion for motorcycles to a new level when he started his Blackhawk Hearse business. For a fitting and dignified last ride, bikers can have their coffins drawn by a Harley Davidson motorbike.

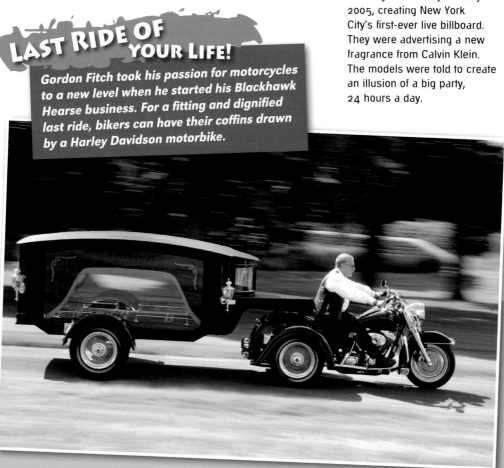

CHOMPING CHAMP

Australian "Bushtucker Freddy" devours a locust during the 2005 Bug Eating Championships. He went on to win the competition that involved challengers from all over the world eating a variety of creepy crawlies, such as crickets, mealworms, hornets, and locusts.

CAR POLISH

You can't miss Yvonne Millner when she drives down the streets of Hopkins, South Carolina—hers is the car decorated in nail polish. She started by painting on a smiling face, but now she has designs and slogans all over her car, including a palm tree and the words "Hang Loose."

She spends three to four hours a day on the creation and has used more than 100 bottles of nail polish.

LONG MUSTACHE

Heads turn when Paul Miller, from Alta Loma, California, walks down the street. That's because his mustache is 10 ft (3 m) long! It takes him an hour to groom it each day.

ACKNOWLEDGMENTS

FRONT COVER (t/l) Natasha Veruschka, (sp) Jim Mouth; 4 (l) Jim Mouth; 5 (l) Natasha Veruschka; 6–7 Leon Schadeberg/Rex Features; 7 Reuters/Chaiwat Subprasom; 8 Ben Philips/Barcroft Media; 9 Craig Barritt/Barcroft Media; 10 Malissa Kusiek/AP/PA Photos; 11 Mark Mirko/Rex Features; 12–13 Jim Mouth; 17 Indranil Mukherjee/AFP/Getty/Getty Images; 18 Reuters/Will Burgess; 20–21 Moses Lanham; 22 Reuters/John Gress; 23 Barcroft Media; 24 Reuters/Toby Melville; 25 Heather Insogna; 26 Natasha Veruschka; 28 Reuters/Alexander Demianchuk; 29 Reuters/Francois Lenoir; 30–31 Jim Mcnitt; 32 Photograph by Ma Qibing/Phototex/Camera Press; 33 Stuart Clarke/Rex Features; 34 Reuters/Kai Pfaffenbach; 36 Gary Roberts/Rex Features; 37 Chinafotopress/Camera Press; 38–39 Simon Burt/Rex Features; 42 Reuters/Chip East; 43 Reuters/Claro Cortes; 44–45 www.JulianCash.com; 46 Doug Hall/Rex Features; 47 Ben Philips/Barcroft Media;

KEY t = top, b = bottom, c = center, l = left, r = right, sp = single page, dp = double page

All other photos are from Ripley's Entertainment Inc.
Every attempt has been made to acknowledge correctly and contact copyright holders and we apologize in advance for any unintentional errors or omissions, which will be corrected in future editions.